SCIENCE ENCYCLOPEDIA
CELLS

An imprint of Om Books International

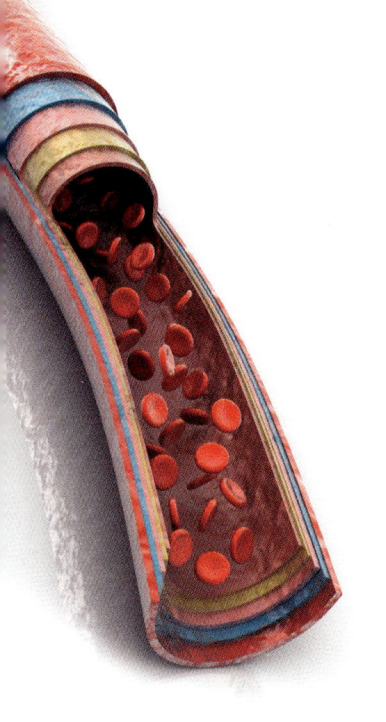

Contents

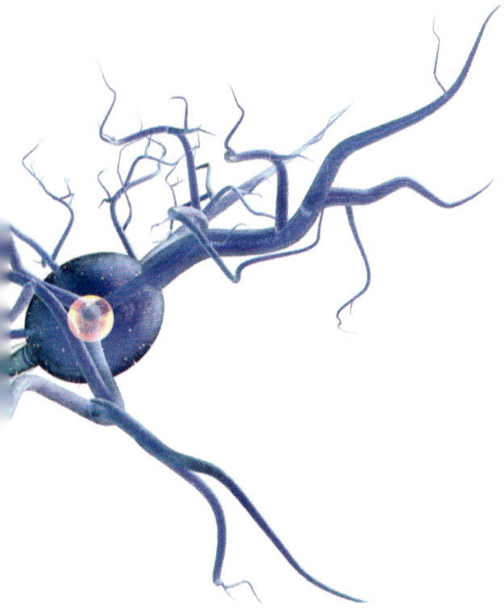

What is Cell Theory?	4
Building Block of Cells	5
Plant Cell and its Structure	6
Life Cycle of a Plant	8
Animal Cell	10
Life Cycle of Animals	12
Muscle	14
Movement	15
Human Body	16
Bones	18
Joints	19
Muscle	20
Movement	21
Nerves	22
Senses	23
Blood and Circulation	24
WBCs and RBCs	25
Nutrition in Plants	26
Respiration	27
Digestion	28
Reproductive System	29
DNA	30
Body Repair	32

CELLS

A cell is the smallest unit of life. Every structural part of a human, animal, plant and organism is composed of cells. Living things range from simple and single-celled to complex and multicellular, such as human beings. Our human body comprises trillions of cells. These cells make up the structure of the body, absorb nutrients from food, convert these nutrients into energy and perform specialised functions.

Cells also contain the body's hereditary material and can make copies of themselves.

The study of cells began approximately 330 years ago. Robert Hooke was the first person to discover cells and coined the term "cells". In 1838, German botanist Matthias Schleiden found that all plants have cells as their basic unit. Around a year later, German zoologist Theodor Schwann discovered that all animals also have cells as the basic unit of life. In 1855, German physician Rudolph Virchow also contributed to this theory, when he found that all cells come from other existing cells.

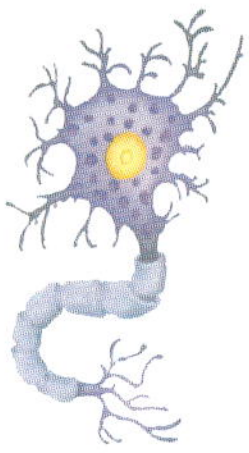

SCIENCE ENCYCLOPEDIA

What is Cell Theory?

In 1838, German botanist Matthias Schleiden discovered that all plants were composed of cells. Subsequently, a year later, German zoologist Theodor Schwann discovered that all animals were composed of cells as well. These two scientists proposed the cell theory.

The basic unit

The first part of cell theory explains that all living things can be very simple, that is, composed of just one cell. There are varied structures within the single-celled amoeba that help it to reproduce, use the energy for growth, respond to the environment and let nutrients and materials enter and exit the cell. Larger organisms, such as a cat or coconut tree, are also composed of cells. If you observe a small tissue sample under a microscope, you will see one actual cell within the larger living thing. Thus, cells reproduce to form new cells, thereby explaining how organisms reproduce and grow. For example, the human skin is constantly being replenished as new cells replace the old ones. If you use a dry towel to rub down your body after a warm bath, you will see old tissue fall off your skin. This tissue is made up of millions of tiny, dead cells.

If we magnify our skin under a powerful microscope, we will be able to see cell tissues.

Modern interpretation of the cell theory

The generally accepted parts of modern cell theory include:

- All known living creatures are made up of single or more cells.

- All living cells are formed from pre-existing cells by the method of division.

- The cell is the most fundamental unit of any structure in all living organisms.

- The different activities of organisms depend on the total activities of independent cells.

- Energy flow occurs within the cells.

- Cells contain deoxyribonucleic acid (DNA), which is found specifically in the chromosome and ribonucleic acid (RNA), which is found in the cell nucleus and cytoplasm.

- All cells are basically the same with respect to the chemical composition in organisms of similar species.

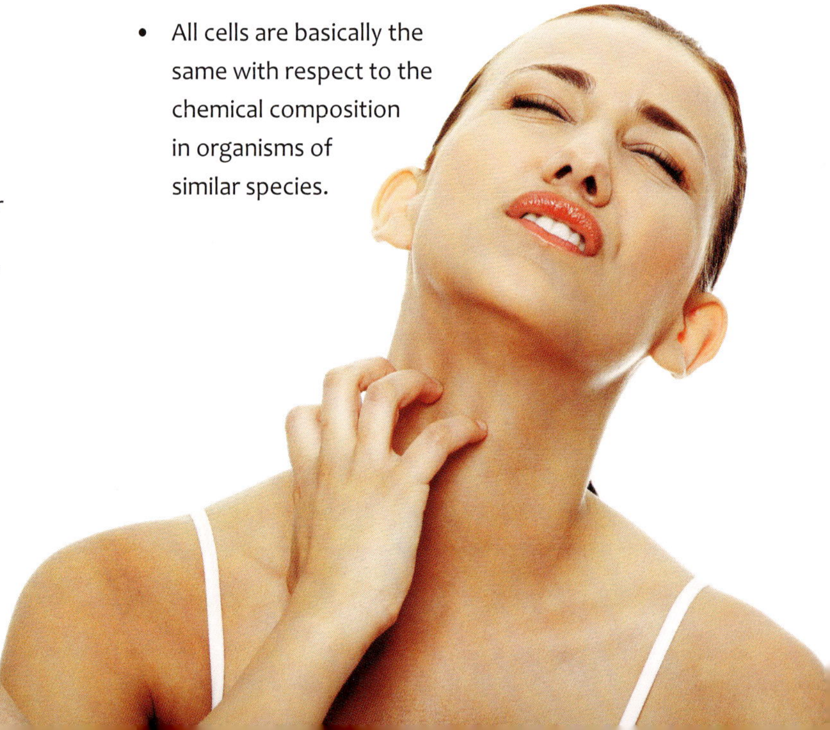

Building Block of Cells

Cell is the basic unit of living organisms. Just like a building stands by joining many bricks, our body is formed by different types of trillions of cells joined together.

What are these cells? What are they made up of? All cells are composed of some common building blocks, regardless of whether they are plant cells or animal cells or whether they have a different function or location. These building blocks are called biomolecules.

Carbohydrates

These are the major source of energy in our body. The most common carbohydrate is sugar. Carbohydrates provide structure and help in the defence mechanism of any cell. They also help in communication and adhesion.

Proteins

Different amino acids join together and form different types of proteins. We all know that protein is a body building constituent. Besides this, proteins are useful in cell transport, maintaining cell contact and controlling its activity. Membrane proteins can also function as enzymes to accelerate chemical reactions, act as receptors for specific molecules, or transport materials across the cell membrane.

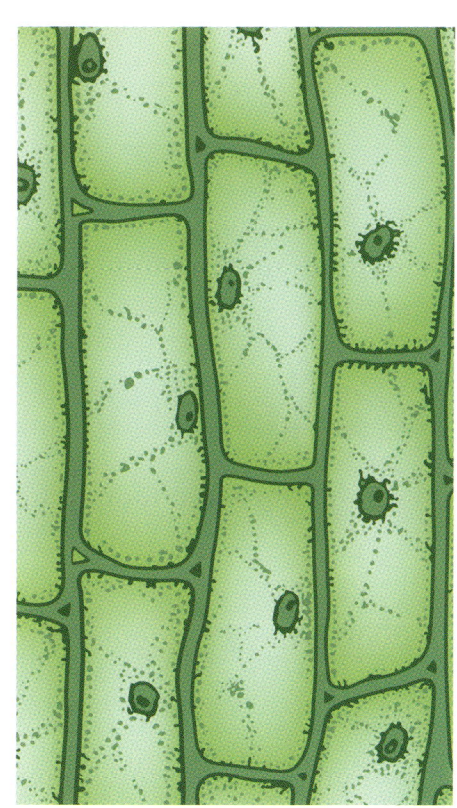
Microscopic view of a plant cell showing anatomical structures.

Lipids

A range of fats, oils, waxes and steroid hormones come under lipids that form cells. Fats also serve as a source of energy and form the cell membrane. These materials provide protection against microbes. Lipids in the form of steroid hormones regulate cell activity.

Nucleic acids

There are two types of nucleic acids found in our body. They are RNA and DNA. DNA is found in the nucleus and it carries genetic information, whereas RNA helps in protein synthesis. It is transcribed from the DNA.

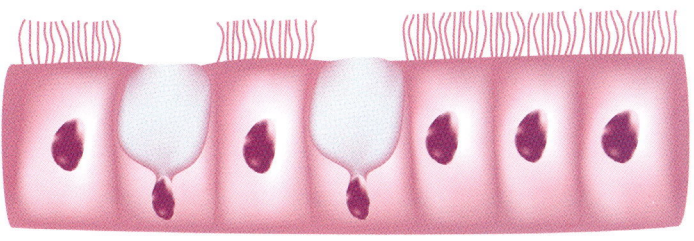
Microscopic view of an animal cell showing anatomical structures.

Cells divide and re-divide to help a plant grow.

SCIENCE ENCYCLOPEDIA

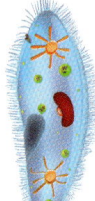

Plant Cell and its Structure

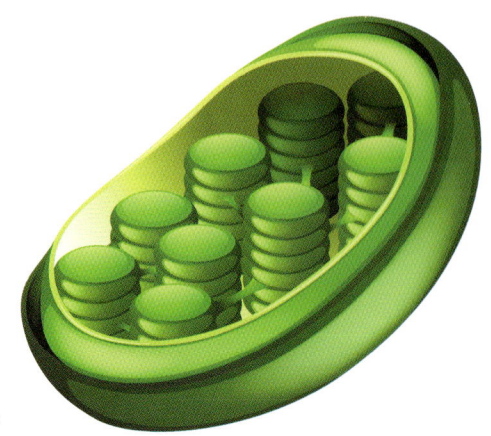

There are two major types of cells: plant cells and animal cells. There are a lot of differences between plant and animal cells. Plant cells are covered by a thick cell wall to give them rigidity. A plant cell can also produce its own food.

Distinctive features of plant cells

1. These cells have a large vacuole filled with water and other materials and surrounded by a membrane called tonoplast. It helps in storing and digesting materials, controlling the movement of molecules and maintaining the cell's turgor.

2. These cells are covered with a thick cell wall made up of cellulose.

3. They have plasmodesmata, which are the pores in the cell membrane.

4. Plastids like chloroplast, amyloplast, chromoplast and elaioplast are present. Chloroplast contains a green pigment called chlorophyll present in the leaves that absorbs sunlight and water, and helps in making food for the plant. This process is called photosynthesis.

5. Cell division occurs in the presence of phragmoplast.

FUN FACT

Chocolate releases the hormone serotonin in the human body that makes you feel relaxed, calm and happy.

A dose of laughter can suppress the release of stress hormones like cortisol and epinephrine.

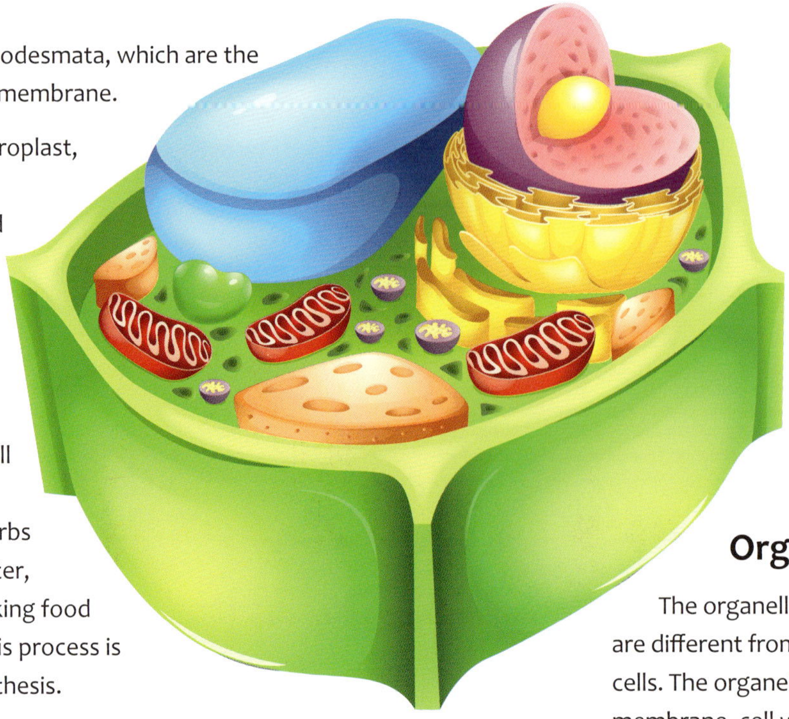

Plant cell showing anatomical structures.

Organelles

The organelles present in plant cells are different from that present in animal cells. The organelles of plant cells are cell membrane, cell wall, nuclear membrane, plasmodesma, vacuole, plastids, chloroplast, leucoplast, chrome-plated Golgi bodies, cytoplasm, nucleus, DNA, chromatin, RNA, cytoskeleton, nucleolus and mitochondrion. If you want to distinguish between animal cells and plant cells, it is very apparent. Plant cells have a particular shape and are not irregularly shaped like animal cells.

Types of plant cells

- Parenchyma cells
- Collenchyma cells
- Sclerenchyma cells

Leaf surface showing plant cells.

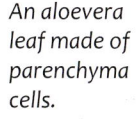

Parenchyma cells

These cells have thin, permeable cell membranes that are found in vascular bundles of the phloem and xylem. The same cell system is also found in leaves. Some parenchyma cells present in the stem are specialised for the absorption of light and providing support for gaseous exchange while some others are non-specialised and remain deep inside the body. Some of these cells, which possess chlorophyll, are called chlorenchyma cells. These cells perform most of the metabolic processes of the plant and also perform other functions like storage, transferring nutrients and water, nectar and some other substance secretions. For example, an aloevera leaf belongs to the cactus family and uses photosynthesis to produce energy as well as stores food in bulk.

An aloevera leaf made of parenchyma cells.

Collenchyma cells

These cells are quite elongated in appearance and can undergo division transversely, giving them a separate appearance. These cells are not hard and form the body of the soft stem and support as a plastic stem. These cells are alive at maturity and possess a cell membrane composed of pectin or hemicelluloses, which is tough at the corners.

The bark is made up of sclerenchyma cells.

Sclerenchyma cells

These are the cells that provide mechanical support to the plant in standing erect for a long time. They are the hard and tough cells of the plant. They are further divided into two types: sclereids and fibres. These cells die at maturity. They secrete a hard cell wall inside the primary cell wall that restricts the exchange of materials and water, giving them a short lifespan. For example, if you closely observe the bark of a tree, you will find that it has all the characteristics that sclerenchyma cells impart to it. The bark of a tree is tough and dry. A bark is made up of dead cells of the tree. These cells dehydrate and become hard, and enable the tree to stand erect and tall. If you pour water on this bark, you will realise that it doesn't absorb any and lets it flow to the ground, from where the roots absorb it and send it to the leaf.

A fern consisting of collenchyma cells.

SCIENCE ENCYCLOPEDIA

Life Cycle of a Plant

Among the various systems of living organisms, the reproductive system is one by which an offspring can be produced from a living organism. Like animals, plants also reproduce. In the life cycle of a plant, a flower produces seeds, which can generate many more plants. Plants can be classified into annuals, biennials, perennials and monocarpic, depending upon their life cycle. Plants can reproduce sexually as well as asexually.

Germination

The life cycle of a plant begins with the germination of the seed. As the seed gets favourable conditions, it soon sprouts into a small seedling. Favourable conditions include moist soil, carbon dioxide and sunlight. This seedling then grows and slowly becomes a fully grown mature plant. Then, reproductive organs develop on the plant. These reproductive organs are flowers.

Reproductive parts

A flower is the reproductive organ of the plant. Some flowers have both male and female parts, whereas others may have any one reproductive part. The sterile parts of flowers are called sepals and petals. The main reproductive part of the flower is the stamen (male, also termed androecium) and carpel (female, also termed gynoecium). Each individual unit of the androecium is called a stamen that consists of a filament, which supports the anther. Pollen grains contain the male gametophyte (microgametophyte) phase of the plant. The gynoecium consists of the stigma, style and ovary which contains one or more ovules. These three structures are often referred to as a pistil or carpel. In many plants, the pistils will fuse for all or part of their length.

Anther
Stigma
Petal
Sepal

In case of flowers that have both male and female parts, pollen grains adhere to the stigma, a pollen tube grows and penetrates the ovule and fertilizes them. The cells then begin to divide. If the flowers have separate sexes, the plant has to depend on external features for the pollen to reach the ovules.

Pollination

After the plant matures, it is the time of pollination. Pollination is the process by which pollen reach into the mouth of the pistil. It makes us wonder how it is possible for pollination to take place as plants can't move like other living organisms. This process needs the help of insects, flies and bees for its completion. They visit the flowers to get nectar, during which the pollen sticks on their wings, legs and other body parts. When they go to another flower, they leave those pollen on the second flower. In this manner, pollen reach the ovary of female flowers and fertilisation occurs.

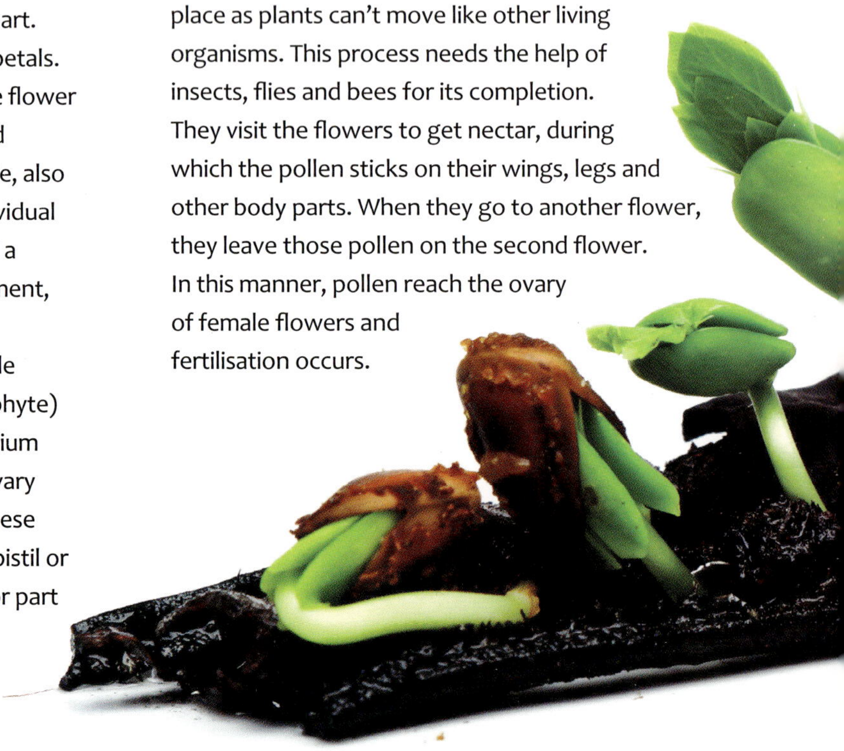

Fertilisation

Fertilisation is defined as the fusion of a male and female gamete to produce a zygote or baby seed. When a flower is fertilised, its ovary begins to swell. The petals wither and fall off the flower. Soon, only the swollen ovary is left. This is the ovary that is known to us as a fruit. The fruit is fleshy on the inside as it holds a lot of nutrition as well as many seeds, which can sprout many more plants. The outer covering of the fruit protects the newly created seed as well as nourishes it.

Dispersal by explosion.

Dispersal of seeds

There are three ways in which seeds get dispersed. The seeds are carried far and wide by water, air, explosion and animals, where they ultimately find soil and favourable conditions, and germinate. Dispersal by water happens when the seed or fruit of a tree falls in flowing water and gets carried away; for example, the coconut. Dispersal by air happens when the seed gets blown away by the wind; for example, the dandelion. Dispersal by explosion happens when the fruit ripens too much, dries up and ultimately, bursts open and throws out all the seeds within it; for example, balsam. Lastly, dispersal by animals is when the seeds stick onto animal fur, or when birds eat the seed and their droppings are found elsewhere, or even when we eat the fruit and throw the seeds away.

Life cycle of some other non-flowering plants

There are different life cycles for non-flowering plants. In gymnosperms, their seeds are open to the air with no layer, such as the seeds of flowering plants. Conifers use cones to store their seeds. Conifers reproduce using their cones. Spores produce spores instead of seeds to reproduce. Mosses typically only grow a few inches tall and use spores to reproduce. Ferns also reproduce using spore casings on the underside of their leaves.

Dispersal by water.

The stages that a seed goes through while germinating.

FUN FACT

The attractive colours of flowers and the sweet scent that they produce, are means by which they attract birds and bees that help in pollination.

SCIENCE ENCYCLOPEDIA

Animal Cell

In 1838, German zoologist, Theodor Schwann discovered that all animals have cell as their basic unit of life. In 1855, German physician Rudolph Virchow also contributed to this theory, when he found that all cells come from other existing cells.

An overview

What makes animals different from any other living organism? They can move around on their own. They can hunt, eat, sleep and make noise. There are so many things that they can do that plants cannot. What gives animals their unique characteristics? It is their cell structure and its constituents that make a difference. The cells present in animals are eukaryotic cells or cells with a membrane-bound nucleus. DNA in animal cells is situated within the nucleus. Animal cells have various sizes and irregular shapes. Most of the cell sizes range between 1 and 100 micrometers and are visible to the human eye only with the help of a microscope.

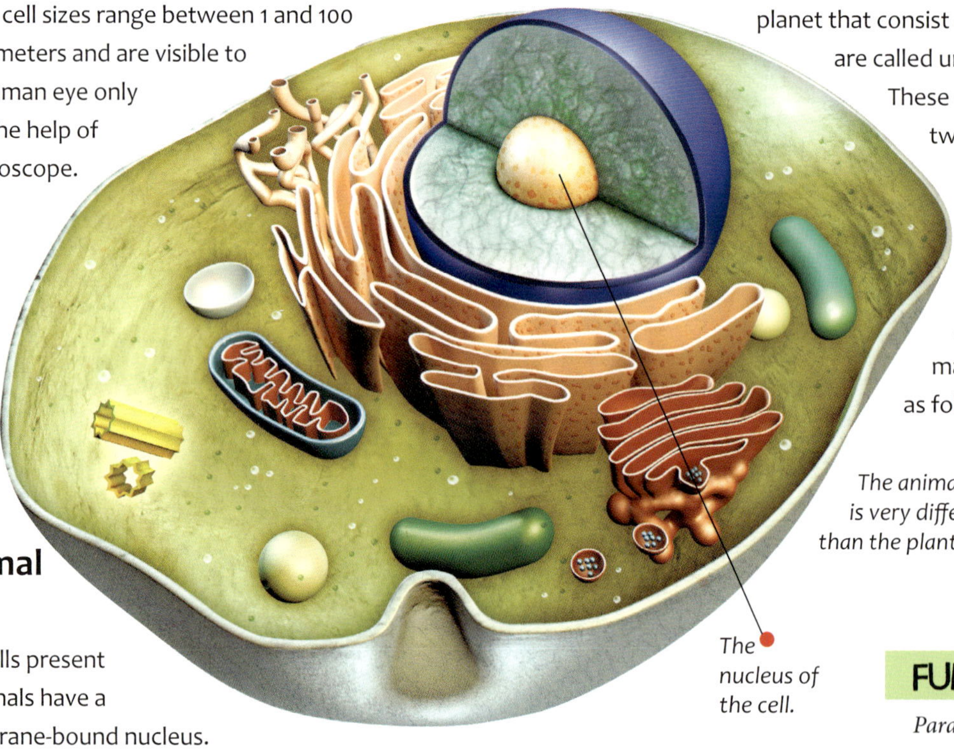

Unicellular animals

What is the smallest animal that we know? Numerous animals come to our mind. The smallest animals that our mind can imagine are insects. However, there are animals that are no more than one cell big. These are only visible to the eyes through a microscope. There are animals on this planet that consist of only one cell. These are called unicellular organisms. These can be classified into two types – Prokaryotes and Eukaryotes. We will look at some examples of Eukaryotic unicellular animals. These are many. Some of them are as follows:

The animal cell is very different than the plant cell.

Animal cell

The cells present in animals have a membrane-bound nucleus. The DNA exists within this nucleus. Also, animal cells contain other membrane-bound organelles that perform specific functions essential for normal cellular operation. Organelles have an extensive range of responsibilities that include everything from producing hormones and enzymes to providing energy for animal cells.

The nucleus of the cell.

FUN FACT

Paramecium is considered as an animal, although it is a single-cell organism. To survive, paramecium uses a tube and a thread of its body for locomotion.

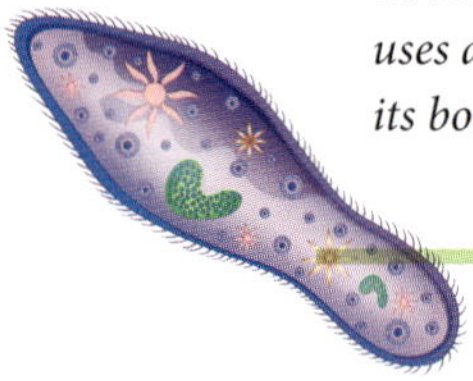

10

CELLS

Paramecium

This unicellular organism is actually neither animal nor plant. However, when learning about unicellular organisms, it is very important to study this organism as it is a model unicellular organism. It has a single mouth that it uses to eat plant as well as small, dead animal cells. It can be found in stagnant water and ponds.

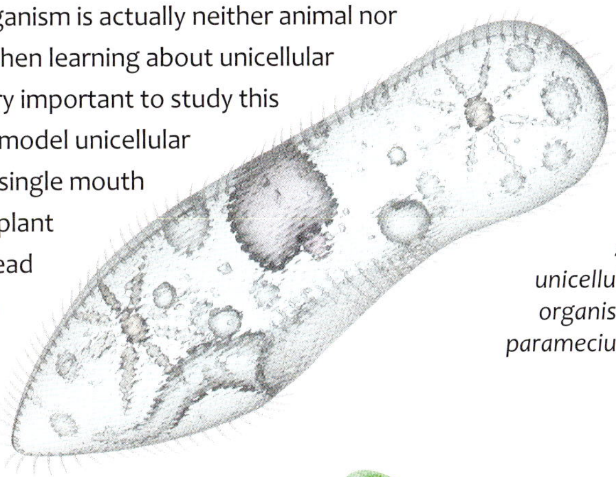

An unicellular organism-paramecium.

Amoeba

Amoeba is a shapeless organism that moves using its ability to take any shape. It basically flows from one spot to another using its flexible boundaries, also known as its pseudopods (false feet). Amoeba is actually plural for Amoeboid. It is unicellular and feeds on bacteria, algae and other microscopic organisms.

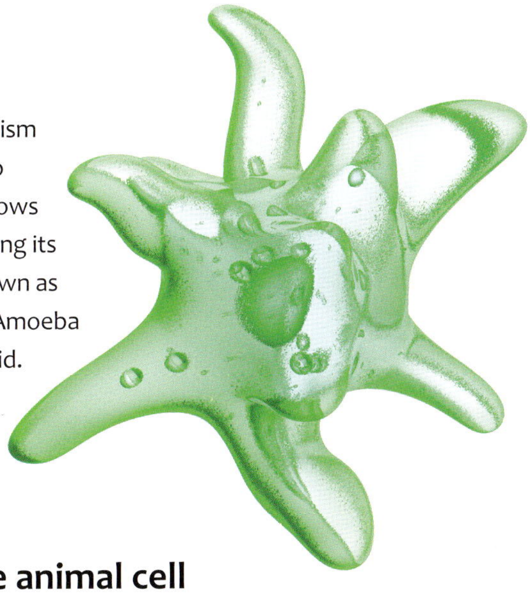

Constituents of the animal cell

Among the species living on this Earth, animals constitute three quarters of the total count. We have already established that these are very different from plants. However, in addition to cell structure, the constituents of cells also make a vast difference in their basic build-up. These cell constituents are called organelles. The ones that animal cells contain are listed below:

Cell membrane	Lysosomes
Centriole	Microfilaments
Cytoplasm	Microtubules
Cilia and flagella	Mitochondria
Endoplasmic reticulum	Nucleus
Endosomes	Peroxisomes
Golgi apparatus	Ribosomes

Scientists have revealed the mystery of the animal cell and disassembled it for further studies and investigations.

Animal cells vs. plant cells

There are many similarities between animal cells and plant cells; the foremost being that they are both eukaryotic cells and have similar organelles. Animal cells are mostly smaller than plant cells. They are also present in various sizes and tend to have irregular shapes, whereas plant cells are more similar in size and are typically rectangular or cube shaped. A plant cell contains structures that are not present in an animal cell. Some of these include a cell wall, a large vacuole and plastids. Plastids, such as chloroplasts, assist in storing and harvesting the needed substances for the plant. In addition, animal cells also contain structures such as centrioles, lysosomes, cilia and flagella that are not ideally present in plant cells.

Making their own food

Of all the differences that we find in a plant and animal cell, the most important one and the one that makes the maximum difference in their existence is the ability to make their own food. Plants can make their own food, whereas animals need to search for it or hunt it. This difference occurs because of the presence and absence of chloroplast in the cells of plants and animals, respectively. It is what gives the plants their green colour. Chloroplast helps the plants to create food from sunlight and CO_2.

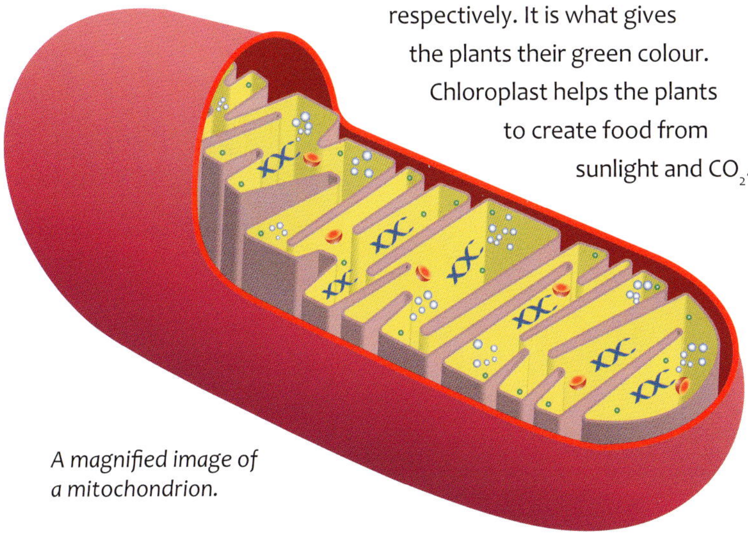

A magnified image of a mitochondrion.

SCIENCE ENCYCLOPEDIA

Life Cycle of Animals

The life cycle of a living organism means the sequence of developmental stages that it passes on its journey towards adulthood. There are thousands of animal species living on Earth, so there are a number of life cycles to observe. In some species, it is a very slow and gradual process, whereas in others, it is fast. For example, the life cycle of some insects is only of a few weeks, whereas the life cycle of sea urchins is many years.

Type of reproduction

Sexual reproduction is found in animals with separate male and female genders. Animals like slugs, snails and barnacles can reproduce asexually. Mammals have a characteristic property of giving birth to young ones, whereas birds, fishes and reptiles are egg-laying animals. In some egg-laying animals like shark, eggs are laid and incubated inside the body, and then given birth to young ones.

Navigating and migrating

Sandhoppers are small, shrimp-like animals that live on sandy beaches. This is their natural habitat. Every 24 hours, they migrate into the sea. They use the Sun to navigate themselves in the direction of the sea and out of it every day. This helps them survive the heat and cold of the day as well as guides them in the correct direction.

CELLS

Insects have a complicated life cycle, which is completed in a few stages, namely, egg, larva, pupa and adult. The larval stage is the stage when most of the feeding is completed. They appear as worms. Subsequently, they form a cocoon and cover their body in it. This is an inactive stage of their life cycle. As the pupa hatches from the cocoon, an adult insect with wings emerges.

Some insects like cockroaches, grasshoppers and dragonflies skip the stage of pupa. They complete their life cycle in three stages – egg, nymph and adult. A nymph is the feeding stage of these insects, after which they change into adults with wings. This is the reason why these species are able to reproduce very fast and create an infestation within a matter of days. As soon as they grow out of their pupal stage, they start moving around in search of food.

The life cycle of a mosquito.

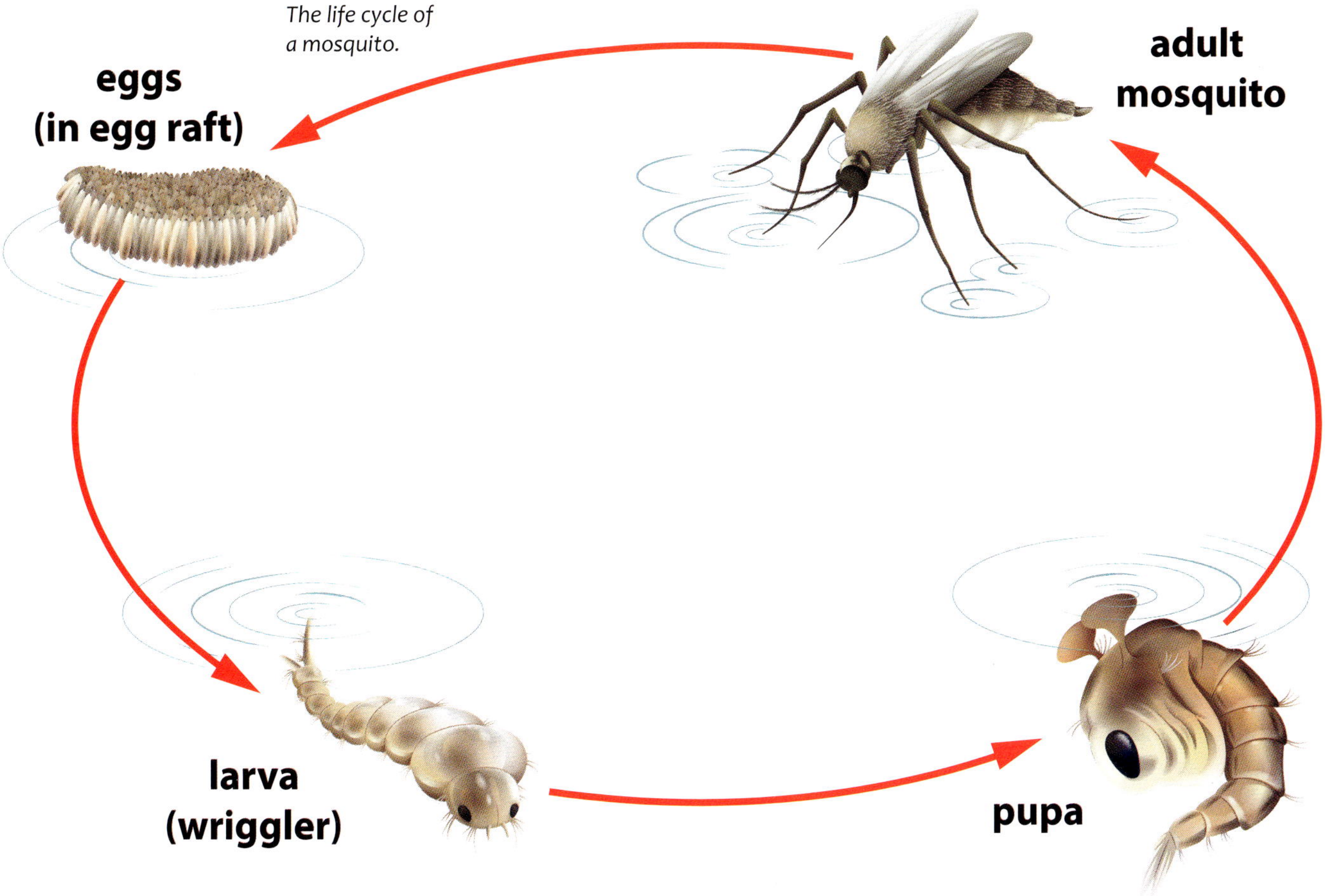

eggs (in egg raft)

adult mosquito

larva (wriggler)

pupa

13

SCIENCE ENCYCLOPEDIA

Amphibians like frogs and newts have a life cycle that completes with a metamorphosis. After their birth, they can swim in water with gills and are called tadpoles that eventually become frogs. After this stage, they change into adults with lungs and can live both on land and water.

The life cycle of a frog.

Adaptation

Environmental conditions like water, temperature and light affect the development of an organism. They have to struggle for food, safety and reproduction; thus, they get adapted to their environment. Animals spend time with other members of the same species. That helps in adaptation. Other examples of animals evolving to adapt to their environment is navigating, migrating, camouflaging and hibernation.

Camouflaging and hibernation

A chameleon is known to be the best example of an animal that uses camouflage to be safe. Chameleons protect themselves from birds of prey by changing their skin colour to that of the background so that they become practically invisible.

Bears are known to hibernate for months during the winters as this helps them conserve their energy and keep warm.

CELLS

Different life cycles

Some animals have very simple life cycles. They are born either from the mother or hatched from an egg to grow into an adult. Fishes, mammals, reptiles and birds have this type of life cycle. Ostrich makes a common nest, in which the male and female both incubate the eggs.

The life cycle of a bee.

Anglerfish

In this species, the tiny male bites the female skin and fertilises the eggs in the female body. When this attachment happens, their bodies fuse to share a circulatory system, so that the female provides nutrients to the male body. The male increases in size as compared to other unattached males. Multiple males can latch onto a female anglerfish at a time.

FUN FACT

The caterpillar attaches to a twig and sheds its outer skin, and within hours, changes into a pupa.

As tadpoles change into frogs, they slowly develop legs and their tail starts shrinking.

Some special life cycles

Virus

As we know, viruses are like parasites on other living organisms. They use host cells, energy and nutrients for nutrition replication. This is very different from symbiosis, where both the organisms benefit from each other. Viruses cause their host's health to deteriorate.

15

SCIENCE ENCYCLOPEDIA

Human Body

The human body is the most intricately working living system. You would be familiar with your body parts, but do you know how many systems are working in your body? The cell is the basic unit of life. Cell combines and forms tissue, which in turn form organs, and these organs together form the structure of the body.

Anatomical structure of human body

The study of the morphology of the human body is called anatomical study. Our body is anatomically divided into many systems as given below:

Skeletal system
Bones, joints and the vertebral column constitute the skeletal system. Major functions performed by this system are support, movement, protection, production of blood cells, endocrine regulation and storage of ions.

Endocrine system
A large collection of ductless glands constitute the endocrine system. Pituitary gland, pineal gland, pancreas, ovaries, testes, thyroid gland, parathyroid gland, hypothalamus, gastrointestinal tract and adrenal gland are the major endocrine glands. They cover a wide range of functions.

Muscular system
The shape of the body is determined by the overall distribution of muscles and fatty tissues. Skeletal, smooth and cardiac muscles constitute this organ system.

Digestive system
Salivary glands, teeth, oesophagus, stomach, small intestine, large intestine, liver and the gall bladder constitute the digestive system.

Homeostasis

Our body maintains homeostasis, meaning it regulates its temperature, pH, blood flow and position at a constant level. Homeostasis is very vital for survival. For example, if the temperature is too high, we tend to sweat profusely. This is how the body gets rid of heat within so that its internal temperature is maintained. Our internal organs are very delicate and hence the temperature and vital levels of the body must be maintained at all times.

Another example is when we eat too much sugar. Our body detects this and sends a signal to our brain, who in turn activates the endocrine system and releases insulin to deal with it.

The cross-section of a sweat gland.

Integumentary system
Skin, hair and nails constitute the integumentary system. This system protects the body from damage, loss of water and abrasions. The study of the working of these systems is called physiology. All the systems in the body are mutually correlated in functioning.

The muscular system of the human body.

Excretory system
Kidney, urinary bladder, ureters and the urethra constitute the excretory system. It removes wastes from the body.

Cardiovascular system
Heart, arteries, veins and capillaries constitute the cardiovascular system. Heart, the pumping organ of the body, circulates blood continuously through the body.

Nervous system
Brain, spinal cord and a network of nerves constitute the nervous system. This system transmits signals from different organs to the brain and vice versa.

Lymphatic system
The lymphatic system is the immune system of the body composed of lymph vessels that form a network in the body.

Reproductive system
The male reproductive parts comprise the penis, testes and the prostate gland. The female reproductive parts comprise the ovary, uterus, fallopian tubes and the vagina. The organ system of the male body and the female body are quite different, also giving them secondary sexual characters.

CELLS

Respiratory system
Lungs, trachea, bronchi, bronchioles and diaphragm constitute the respiratory system. This system is responsible for the intake of oxygen and releasing carbon dioxide out of the body.

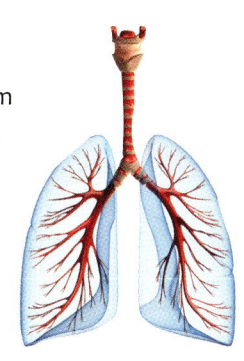

Some facts about the human body

- There are 206 bones in an adult human body. A child has more bones which then fuse as the body grows older.

- The human body can be divided into many body cavities like pelvic cavity, thoracic cavity, abdominal cavity and dorsal cavity. Many small cavities are also there, which are called sinuses.

- The red fluid flowing through the vessels in the body is called blood. An adult human body has 5 to 5.5 l of blood.

- The presence of red blood cells lends blood the red colouration.

- A human body contains about 75 per cent of water.

- The small intestine found in the abdomen is 6 m long.

- The human heart beats at a rate of 73 beats per minute. This is the pulse rate that we feel in our wrist.

- Copper, zinc, cobalt, calcium, manganese, phosphates, nickel and silicon are found in our body in different forms.

- Nose behaves as a natural air conditioner as it changes the temperature of the air received by the body and also removes impurities from it.

SCIENCE ENCYCLOPEDIA

Bones

The branch of science called "biology" studies the structure of the human body. If we touch any part of our body, we will find something hard beneath the muscles. The hard organs are called bones that form the skeleton of the human body. An adult human body is composed of 206 bones that are of different shapes and sizes.

What are bones?

Bones are rigid organs that together constitute the vertebral skeleton. The red and white cells of blood are produced inside these bones. The bones consist of dense connective tissues of cortical and cancellous type. They are light in weight but strong and hard, and store different minerals. The different types of bones are flat, long, short, irregular and sesamoid bones.

Skeleton

In our body, the femur (thigh bone) is the longest bone. The stirrup inside the ear is the smallest bone. Each hand has 26 bones.

Cartilage

The nose and ears are not made of bone but of cartilage. The cartilage is not as hard as the bone and is made out of flexible bone tissue. This is the reason why we can squish our nose and bend our ears without breaking them.

Joints

If bones are so hard, how can we bend our hands or legs? Are they flexible too? The answer will be no, as a bone cannot bend. It is the joint that helps us to bend our hand or other parts. We can bend our hand at any point because there are joints like the elbow joint, shoulder joint and wrist joint.

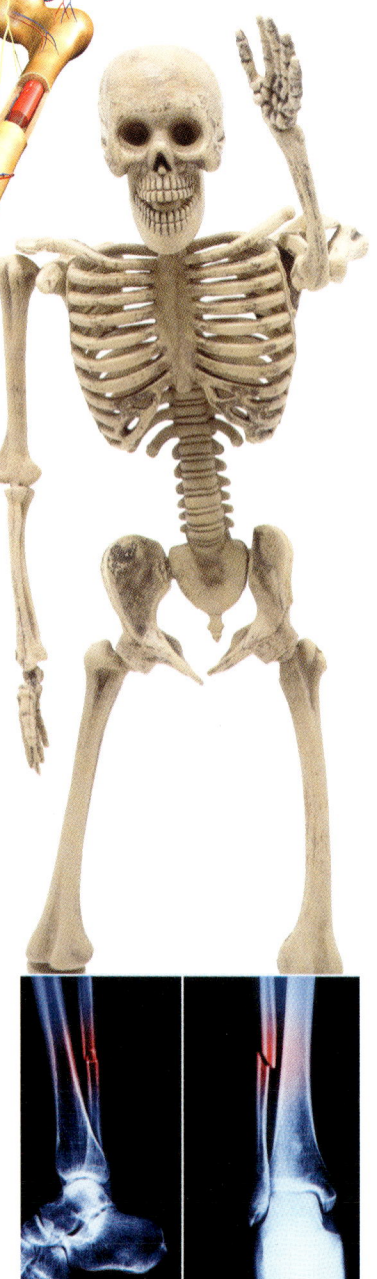

An x-ray of a human with fractured ankles.

Bone injury

When a bone cracks or breaks due to an accident, it is called a fracture. Based upon the type of damage, there are basically two types of fractures. The first one is a hair-line fracture. This type of fracture happens when the impact on the bone is not too high and hence the x-ray of the bone shows only a minor crack. The second type of fracture is called a complete fracture. This ranges from a gap between the crack in the bone to a completely snapped bone. There is also a third issue related to the bone. This is when, due to a strong impact or yank in one of the body parts, the bone slips out of its position. This is known as a dislocation. This can occur at any of the joints. The most common dislocation is of the shoulder, when the arm bone slips out of the socket. Painful as they all may sound, all these types of bone injuries are treatable and with time, can allow us complete use of the injured body part.

Fractures can occur because of car accidents, falls, sport injuries, low bone density, osteoporosis, etc., which causes the weakening of bones.

Joints

The word "joint" is derived from the Latin word Junctura that means junction or joining. Joints, also known as bony articulations, are the strongest point of meeting of two or more bones; they also attach teeth and cartilage in the body with one another. Think what would have happened, if our body would have been composed of a single, rigid bone. We would have been strong, but without any locomotion or movement. That is why joints are vital in our body.

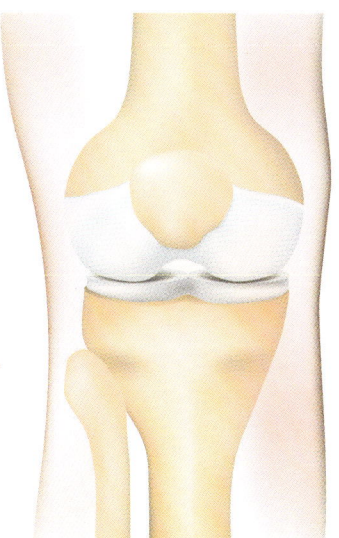

Structure of a joint

A joint is covered by a tough, fibrous capsule, which restricts its motion, and a fluid called synovium present inside the joint capsule, which provides lubrication and prevents friction.

Ligaments are muscles that give strength to the joints and avoid dislocation. Tendons are muscles that attach the bones to other muscles.

Thus, joints are parts of the body that make bending, stretching, twisting and turning activities possible.

Types of joints

Joints can be classified on the basis of their functionality or their structural composition. The functional classification of joints divides them into three types on the basis of the degree of allowed movement.

1. **Synarthrosis**

The joints where no movement is allowed are called synarthroses; for example, the joints in the skull.

2. **Amphiarthrosis**

The joints that allow little movement are called amphiarthroses; for example, the joints in the intervertebral disks of the spine and pubic symphysis of the hips.

3. **Diarthrosis**

The joints that permit a large area for movement are called diarthroses; for example, the joints in the elbow, knee, shoulders and wrists.

Structural classification is based upon the nature of binding tissues and the presence or absence of synovial cavity. On this basis, joints can be of the following types:

1. Fibrous joint
2. Cartilaginous joint
3. Synovial joint

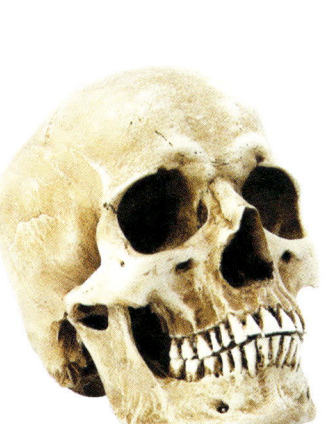

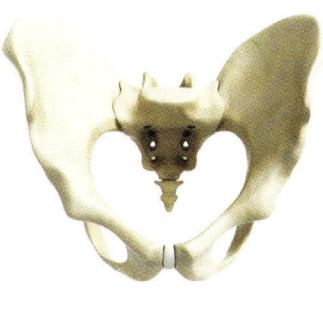

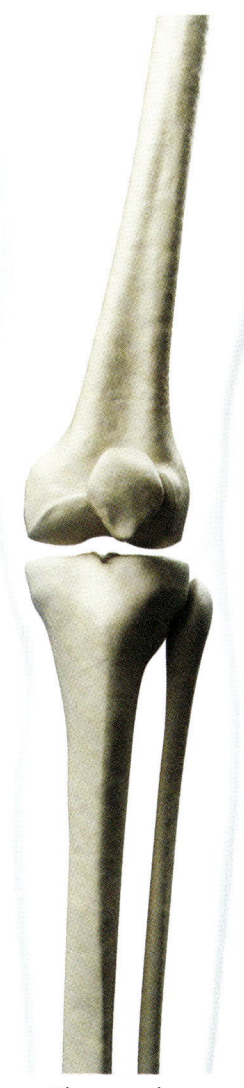

The upper bone is called a femur and the lower two bones are the tibia and fibulla.

SCIENCE ENCYCLOPEDIA

Muscles

A total of 650 muscles constitute the muscular system of the human body. Muscles constitute approximately 70 per cent of our body weight. Our daily life activities like walking, sitting, standing, bending, drinking and eating are all controlled by muscles. There are many other functions of the muscles that go on continuously without our knowledge, like pumping of the heart, breathing with lungs and digestion by peristalsis in the alimentary canal.

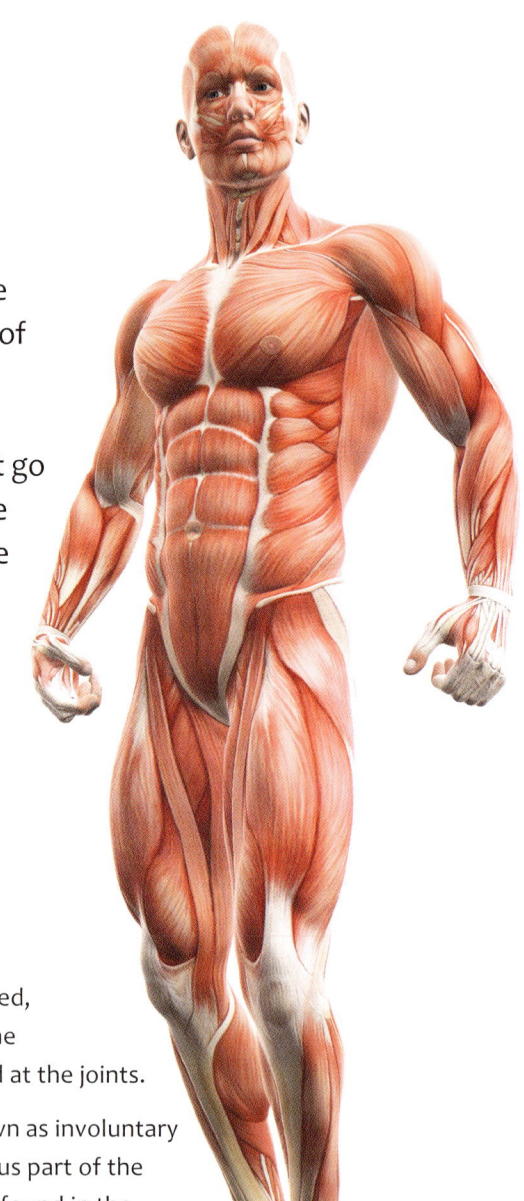

Skeletal muscle.

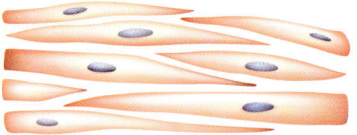
Smooth muscle.

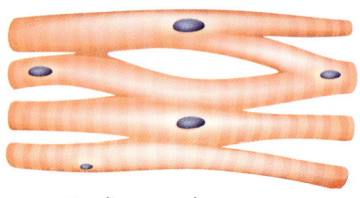
Cardiac muscle.

Types of muscles

There are three types of muscles found in the human body:

1. Skeletal muscles
2. Smooth muscles
3. Cardiac muscles

Skeletal muscles – Skeletal muscles are the striated, voluntary muscles of our body. They control all the consciously performed activities. These are found at the joints.

Smooth muscles – Smooth muscles are also known as involuntary muscles as these are controlled by the unconscious part of the brain. These muscles are spindle-shaped muscles found in the visceral organs of the body. Their wave-like actions generate peristalsis movement and help in passing food, blood, urine, and air from one organ to another.

Cardiac muscles – Cardiac muscles are the striated involuntary muscles found in the heart. These types of muscles can generate electrical impulses, which produce rhythmic contractions in the heart.

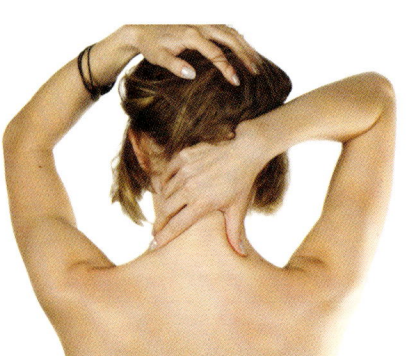

Functions of the muscles

Muscles are the only part of the body possessing the ability to contract. That is why they are necessary for locomotion or movement. Besides this, muscles maintain the posture of the body and transport blood, urine, food and many other substances. Muscles are also responsible for generating body heat.

How muscles get fatigued

Our muscles get fatigued when we work excessively. This is because our muscles use energy from one or the other source of our body to work. During excessive workout, the muscles lack this energy, causing waste products like lactic acid and ADP to get accumulated, thereby making us feel tired. Our muscles feel like they are on fire.

Movement

We have studied that the human body consists of many types of joints, which allow different types of movements. Movement is necessary for the human body to physically move and do a lot of things. By the term "movement", we understand the motion of organs, joints, limbs and other sections of the body. The skeleton of the human body works with 650 muscles to allow all movements.

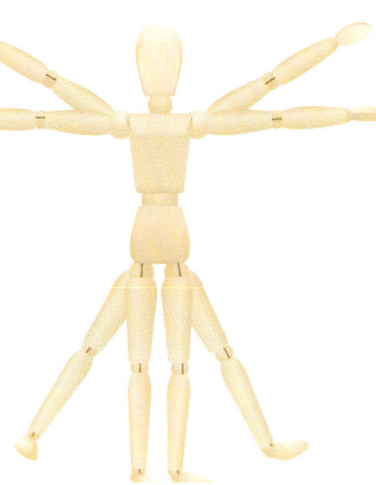

Study of movement

A child learns movements like walking, eating and standing. As he/she grows older, he/she can learn many other activities by practice and skill.

The study of movements is based on the principles of biomechanics and kinesiology. The scientific study of movements is known as kinesiology or human kinetic.

The movement can include the study of gait, posture, sports, exercise movements and daily life activities.

Scientists study the human body in different planes and different anatomical positions. Movements in the joints can be classified into various types considering these planes and positions.

The human body has to make use of multiple and many muscles while running.

We use the muscles of our back and stomach to bend over and touch our toes.

Different types of movements

The different types of movements that are allowed through various angles at various joints are flexion, extension, abduction, adduction, horizontal abduction, horizontal adduction, internal rotation, external adduction, lateral flexion, rotation, elevation, depression, retraction, protraction, upward rotation, downward rotation, circumduction, radial deviation, ulnar deviation, opposition, eversion, inversion, dorsiflexion, plantar flexion, pronation and supination.

Movements can also be classified in various categories based on the nature of the joints involved like gliding, angular and rotational movements. Movements can be either of linear or angular type.

For example, the movement of our wrist from side to side is a gliding movement, the movement of our elbow while flexing our muscles is an angular movement and our head rotating at the neck is a rotational movement.

21

SCIENCE ENCYCLOPEDIA

Nerves

Nerves are a collection of cells called neurons. Nerves are studied under the nervous system, which is responsible for all voluntary and involuntary actions, and for every movement, sensation and thought. There are approximately 100 billion nerves in the peripheral nervous system.

If we touch a bowl that is very hot, we spontaneously remove our hand. This occurs within seconds and we don't need to think about it. Such actions are done because of nerves.

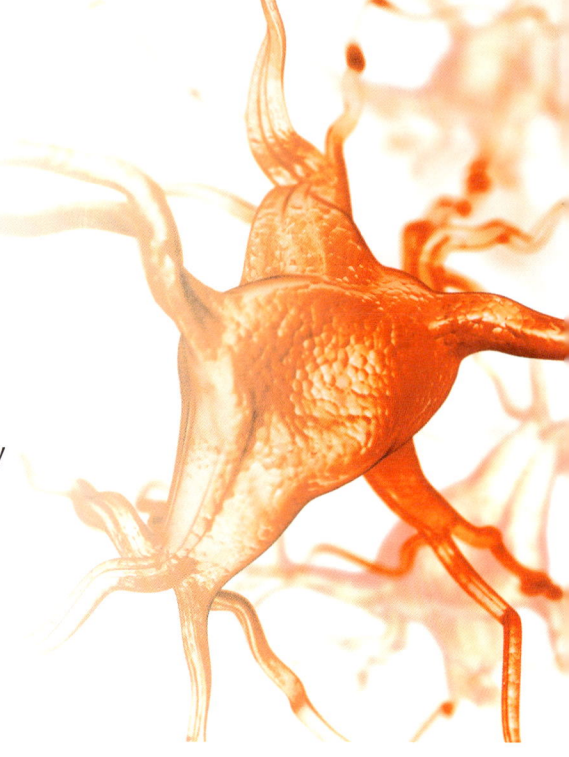

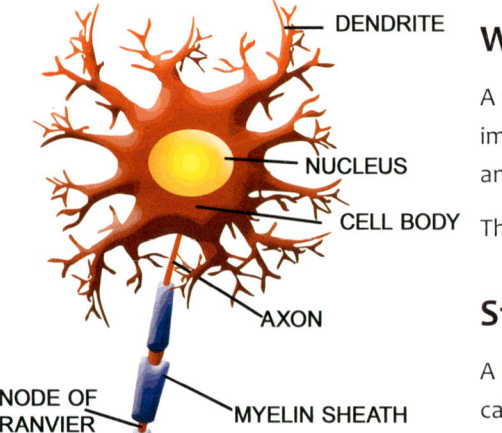

What is a nerve?

A nerve is a specialised cell or cord-like bundle of fibres that transmits nerve impulses in the form of electrochemical signals from different organs to the brain and from the brain to different organs and body parts.

The term used for diseases related to nerves is neuropathy.

Structure

A neuron comprises a large cell body with one elongated axon and many branches called dendrites. They are surrounded by the Schwann cells in the peripheral nervous system. The axon is surrounded by multi-layered sheath called myelin and/or a membrane called neurilemma. The nerve carries information in the form of electrochemical impulses at a speed of 120 m/s. The junction between two neurons is called the synapse.

Types

There are three types of nerves based on the direction of the electrical signals they carry.

1. **Sensory nerves:** These nerves transmit impulses from the sensory organs to the brain.

For example, when we touch a hot utensil by mistake, the sensory nerves from the skin of our hands send signals to our brain.

2. **Motor nerves:** These nerves transmit impulses from the brain to organs, glands and muscles.

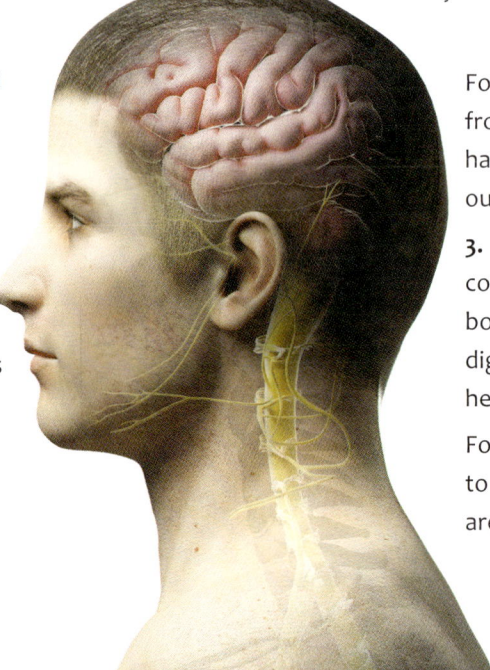

The brain is the headquarter of our nervous system.

For example, on getting a message from our hand, the brain signals the hand to move it back and we retract our hand.

3. **Autonomic nerves:** These nerves control involuntary actions of the body like temperature regulation, digestion, blood pressure and heart rate.

For example, our heart beats faster to pump more blood when we are active.

22

Senses

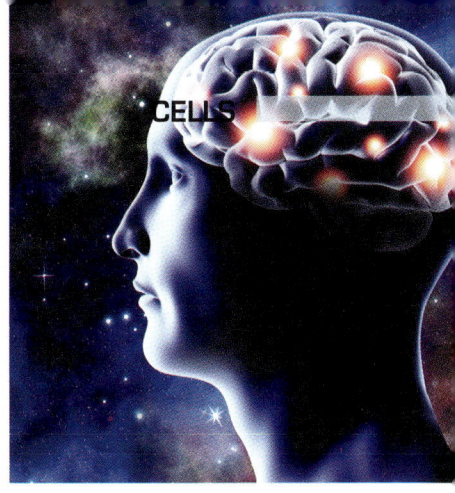

Aristotle described that there are five sense organs present in the human body. Sense is the physiological capacity of an organism to react to some external stimuli. The five senses that a human body has are smell, sight, sound, taste and touch.

The famous five

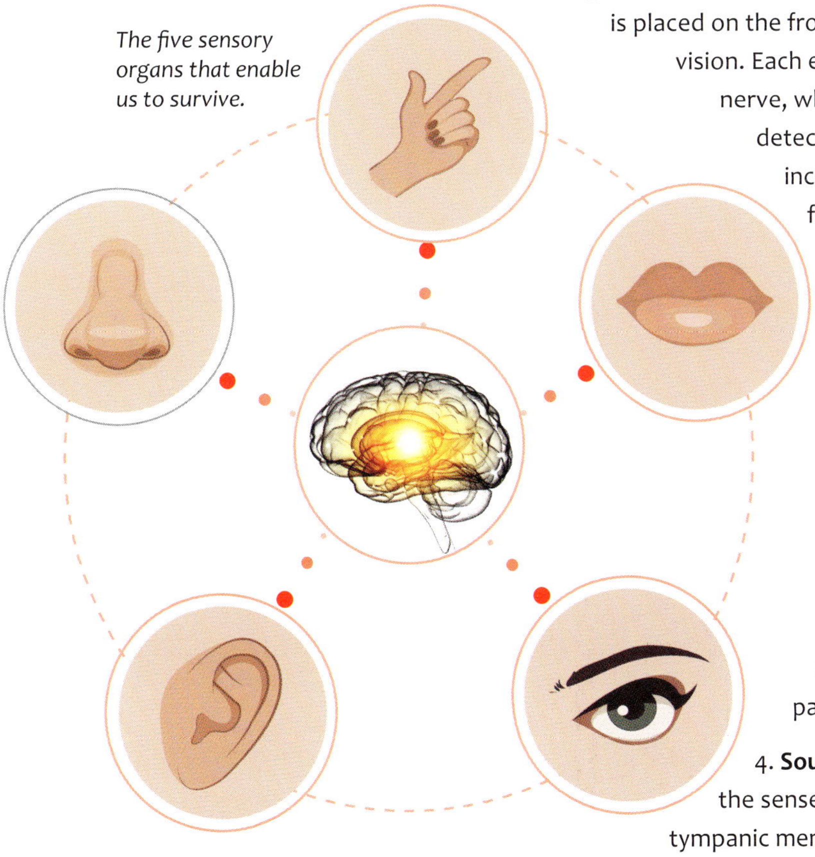

The five sensory organs that enable us to survive.

1. **Seeing:** A human being possesses a pair of eyes for visual perception. This is placed on the front side of our head to allow a maximum range of vision. Each eye remains connected to the brain by the optic nerve, which gives electrical impulses to the brain for detecting and forming images. Different parts of the eye include lens, conjunctiva, retina, pupil, cornea, iris and fovea. Our eyes have photoreceptor cells in them. Rods and cones are the two photoreceptor cells present in the eye.

2. **Smell:** The nose is an organ that detects smell or olfaction. It has hundreds of small olfactory receptors that get excited and signal the brain. Our brain can store memories with respect to different smells. This is why we can recognise smells.

3. **Taste:** Tongue is the sense organ of taste that has taste buds present on it for differentiating between various tastes like bitter, sour, sweet and salty. We taste these different tastes at different parts of the tongue.

4. **Sound:** Two ears present on the sides of the head are the sense organs for hearing or sound perception. There is a tympanic membrane in the ear that vibrates on hearing a sound. These vibrations reach the small bones of the internal ear that sends signals to our brain and enables us to hear sounds.

5. **Touch:** This is a perception that results from the excitation of the minute hair and various nerve endings present all over the body that communicate with the brain.

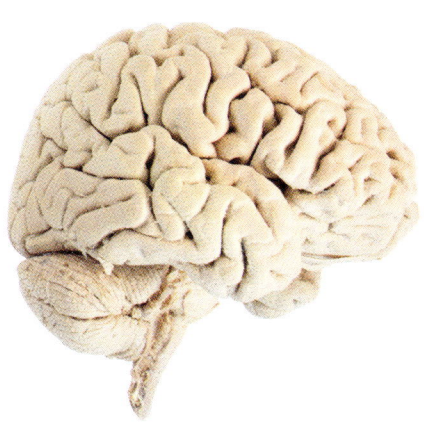

More than five

Besides these five senses, there are many other senses by which a human body can react to many changes in the environment, like temperature, pain, balance, vibration, time, thirst, hunger and many other internal stimuli.

The big boss

Brain has the capacity for perceiving, interpreting and organising the data received by sense organs. Sensing initially occurs at the cellular level, which then goes to the brain by the nervous system.

SCIENCE ENCYCLOPEDIA

Blood and Circulation

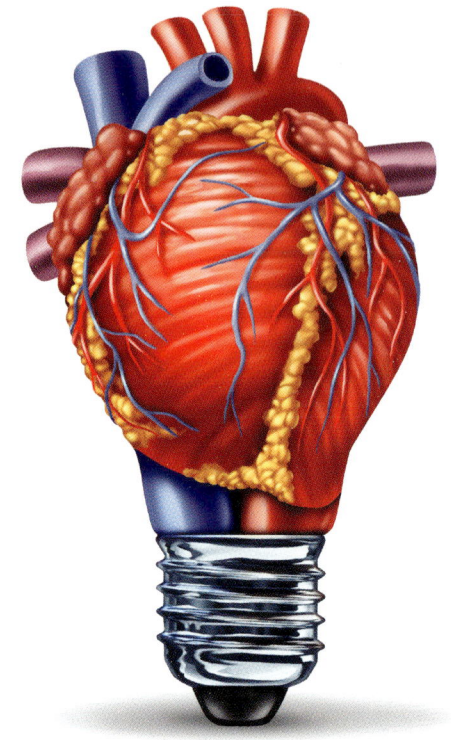

The circulatory system of the body includes the heart, lungs, arteries, veins, capillaries, coronary vessels and blood. This system facilitates the to and fro movement of nutrients, gases, blood as well as hormones.

When you are unwell, your doctor some times advices a blood test. What does this blood removed from your body look like? It doesn't look like water; it gets separated into a layer of pale liquid plasma and a solid layer of blood cells.

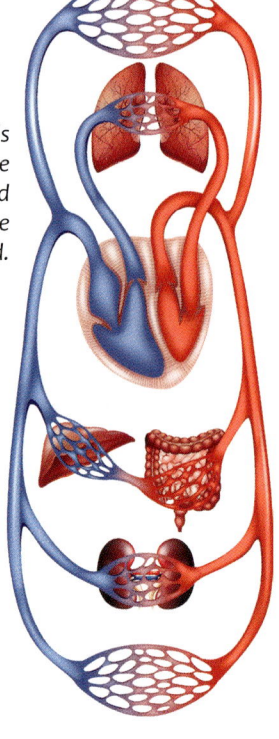

The blue vessels indicate impure blood and red vessels indicate pure blood.

Constitution of blood

Blood constitutes 55 per cent plasma and 45 per cent blood cells.

Different types of blood cells are produced in the bone marrow of human beings by a process known as haematopoiesis.

Plasma: The plasma is a liquid containing water, proteins, glucose and nutrients. It performs the function of transportation.

Red blood cells (RBCs): Red blood cells possess the red pigment haemoglobin, which carries oxygen.

White blood cells (WBCs): White blood cells help in fighting against infections.

Platelets: Platelets help in clot formation, thus preventing bleeding.

Inhaling oxygen.

Blood circulation

Blood circulates in the body through arteries, veins and capillaries. The heart acts as a pump and makes the blood flow through the blood vessels. There are two types of circulation that simultaneously occur in the body. One is the systemic circulation by which organs, tissues and cells get a supply of oxygen-rich blood by the vessels coming from the left ventricle of the heart. Another is the pulmonary circulation by which oxygen inhaled by the lungs enters blood and carbon dioxide is released.

CELLS

WBCs and RBCs

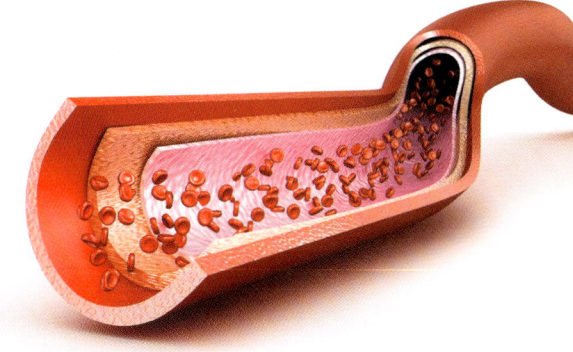

The blood is the most important connective tissue in the human body. It consists of a pale liquid part, the plasma and many blood cells.

Red blood cells

Red blood cells, also called as erythrocytes, are non-nucleated, biconcave disc-shaped cells. RBC is the most abundant cell in the blood and makes up to 40 per cent of the total blood's volume.

Have you ever wondered why blood is always red in colour not white or yellow? This is because of the presence of a protein called haemoglobin. Haemoglobin is a respiratory pigment, mainly composed of iron, which binds with either oxygen or carbon dioxide and helps in their transportation.

These cells are produced inside the bone marrow with the help of the hormone erythropoietin. After seven days of their production, mature RBCs enter into the bloodstream. As these cells are non-nucleated, they give more space to the haemoglobin and facilitate their easy movement across small blood vessels. This property, besides giving them flexibility, decreases their lifespan to 120 days.

Functions

1. Transportation of oxygen and carbon dioxide
2. Maintenance of homeostasis

White blood cells

White blood cells, also known as leukocytes, are irregularly shaped, nucleated cells with a short life span of about three–four days. They constitute only one per cent of the blood.

Based on the presence or absence of cytoplasmic granules, they are classified into two groups: granulocytes and agranulocytes. Neutrophils, eosinophils and basophils are granulocytes and lymphocytes and monocytes are agranulocytes.

Functions

1. They are our bodyguards as they fight infections. They produce a special protein called antibodies for fighting various foreign elements.

2. They develop the immunity of our body.

Besides these cells, platelets are also present in the blood that help in the coagulation of blood.

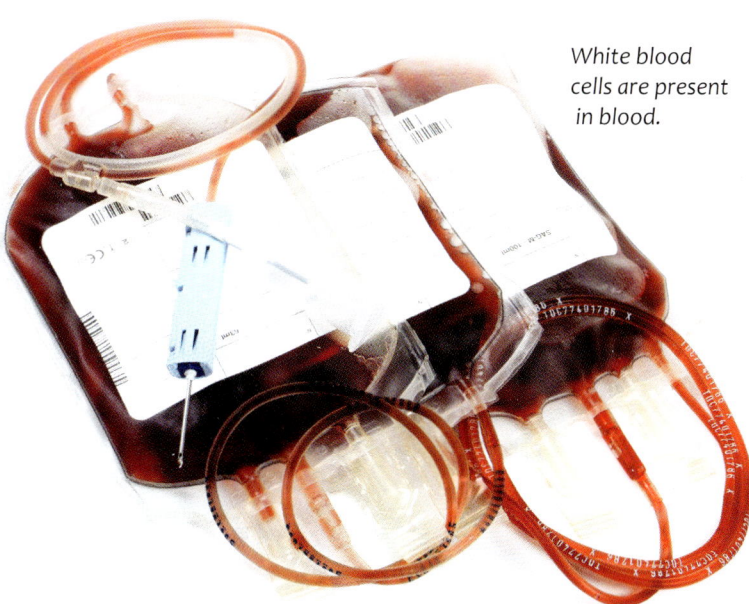

White blood cells are present in blood.

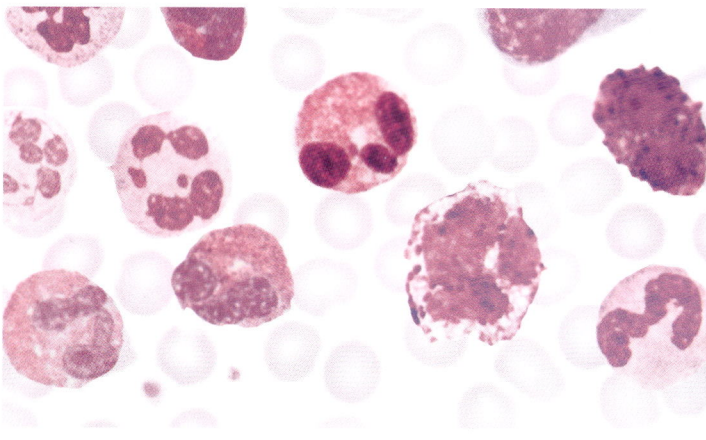

White blood cells.

25

SCIENCE ENCYCLOPEDIA

Nutrition in Plants

One of the most important and basic things required by all living organisms is food. The components of food are proteins, minerals, carbohydrates, vitamins and fats. For all living things, all of these components are very significant. All plants and animals require food for their growth and energy.

Photosynthesis

The mode of nutrition used by plants is known as photosynthesis. Plants make food for themselves with the help of chlorophyll; the items required by plants to make food are sunlight, water and carbon dioxide. Roots absorb water. Leaves take in carbon dioxide from the air and absorb sunlight with the help of chlorophyll in the leaves. After the process is completed by leaves, they produce carbohydrates and oxygen. Carbohydrates are stored in the leaves as starch and oxygen is released into the atmosphere through the stomata.

Rafflesia or the corpse flower.

Modes of nutrition in plants

Substances of chemical nature that provide nourishment to living organism are known as nutrients. Plants are the only organisms on the planet that can make their own food.

Autotrophic nutrition: The word "auto" means "self" and "trophos" means nourishment. Some plants are called autotrophs because they can make their own food. Plants that convert carbon dioxide, water and nutrients into food with the help of photosynthesis are known as autotrophs, and this mode of nutrition is called autotrophic nutrition. For example, your normal rose bush creates its own food.

Heterotrophic nutrition: The word "heterotrophic" is a combination of two words; "hetero" meaning others and "trophos" meaning nourishment. Certain plants are incapable of conducting photosynthesis, and they latch onto other plants and organisms for their nutrition. These plants are called heterotrophic plants and this mode of nutrition is called heterotrophic nutrition. Heterotrophic nutrition occurs in two types of plants: parasitic and saprophytic.

Mistletoe is a parasitic plant as it attaches itself to the stem of a healthy plant for nutrition. Mushrooms are saprophytic plants as they feed on dead and decaying plants for nourishment.

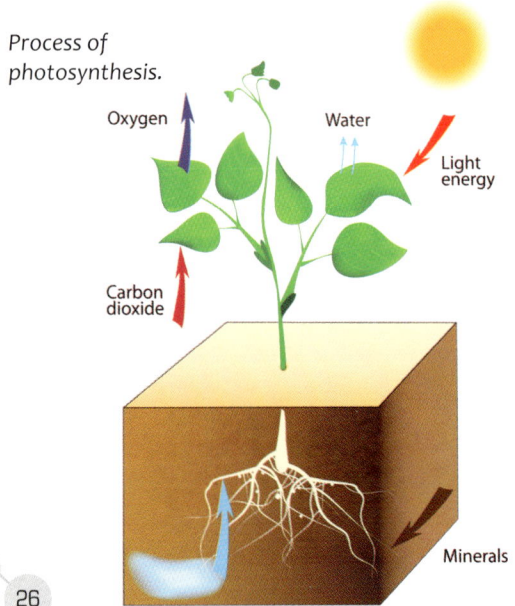

Process of photosynthesis.

CELLS

Respiration

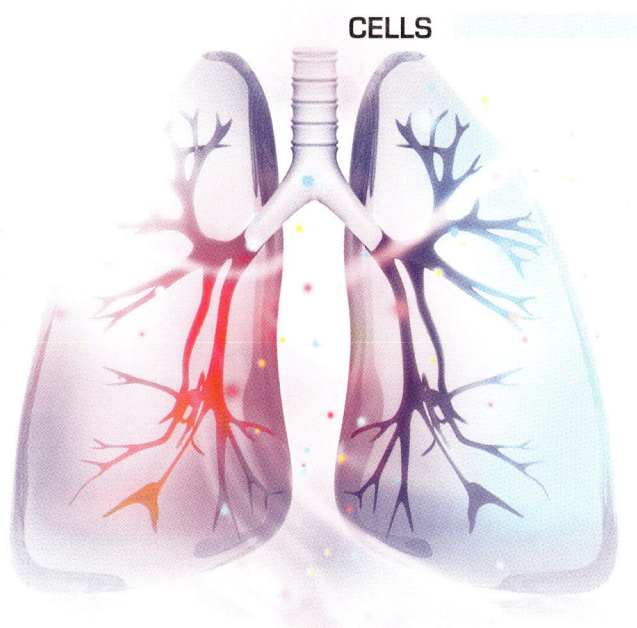

We know that we cannot stay even for a minute with our nose and mouth closed. We need to breathe. It is a process that goes on without our control.

Respiration is the process of taking in oxygen and giving out carbon dioxide into the environment. This can be confused with breathing; however, breathing involves only inhaling and exhaling, and respiration is the process where the gaseous exchange occurs in the cells of the body. The food we eat gives us energy only when it is oxidised, which is achieved by the process of respiration.

Organ system

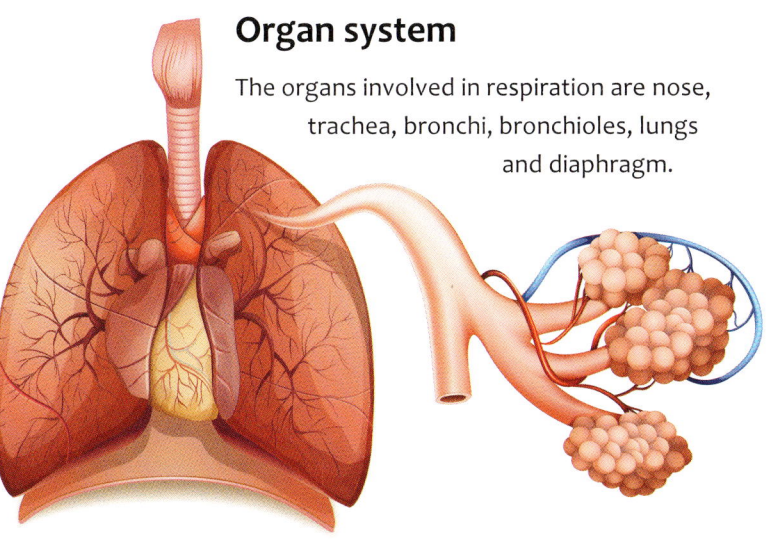

The organs involved in respiration are nose, trachea, bronchi, bronchioles, lungs and diaphragm.

Process of respiration

Lungs are one of the largest organs of the body. In the human body, there are two lungs present in the chest cavity. The gases are exchanged in the alveoli air sacs present in the lungs passively by the process of diffusion. Diaphragm, a membrane-like structure, creates space for the air coming in and pushes the air out of the lungs by its expansions and contractions. Different types of muscles like pectoral muscles, external intercostal muscles and accessory muscles aid in the process of respiration. Nostrils have small hair that act as a filter and remove the dust and dirt from the air that is breathed in.

A man inhaling fresh air through his nose.

Factors affecting respiration

The main factors affecting respiration are temperature, carbon dioxide, light, oxygen, extinction point, water, respiratory substrates, stimulation, climacteric fruits, inhibitors and protoplasmic factors.

When the surface volume ratio is high, the respiration is efficient. As the human body has a large volume, ventilation is required, which affects the process of respiration. The transport pigment called the haemoglobin also plays an important role in the process of respiration.

For example, when your body is doing a heavy workout, blood is pumped faster and hence the rate of respiration also increases.

SCIENCE ENCYCLOPEDIA

Digestion

The digestive system is one of the vital organ systems of our body. It is surprising how digestion actually occurs within the body and how we get energy from food. Food is the essential source of a body to obtain energy, vitamins and minerals. Digestion is the process that changes food into a simpler form, which our cells can absorb.

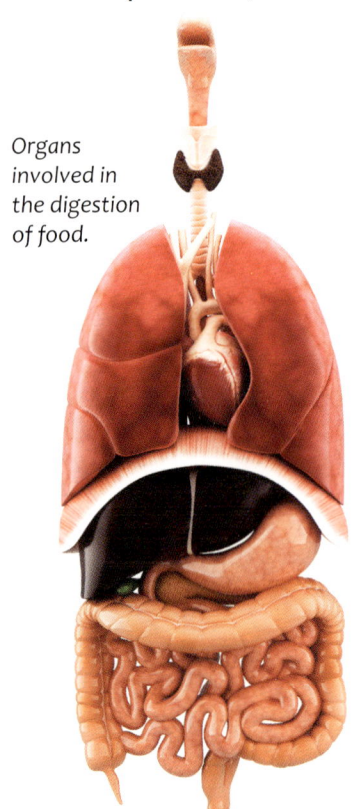

Organs involved in the digestion of food.

Organ system

Different organs involved in the digestive system are teeth, oesophagus, pancreas, stomach, gall bladder, liver, small intestine, large intestine and anus.

The entire passage through which the food journeys, from the mouth to the anus, is called the gastrointestinal tract. It is a 20 to 30-feet-long tube.

Passage of food

Our body prepares itself for the incoming food as soon as we think of eating any food or just smell it. The different steps that food goes through to get digested are as below:

Mastication or chewing: The whole process of digestion starts from the mouth, where the teeth crush and chew food. This process is called the mastication of food. The saliva from the salivary glands mixes with food, forming a semi-liquid mass called bolus. The starch digests at this stage.

Swallowing: This bolus then passes through the oesophagus. In this stage, no digestion occurs and food passes through this pipe by peristalsis movement into the stomach.

Stomach: As food comes to the stomach, it gets mixed with gastric juice, which is mainly composed of pepsin and hydrochloric acid. At this stage, protein digestion occurs.

Small intestine: The food leaving the stomach is called chyme. Chyme enters the duodenum, the first part of the small intestine and mixes with the digestive enzymes coming from the pancreas and liver. At this stage, the remaining digestion occurs.

Large intestine: The food then enters the cecum, colon and rectum. Water and minerals are re-absorbed by the colon, and the waste material goes out of the body through the rectum and a small opening called the anus. The process of removal of waste products is called defecation. The alimentary canal prevents the back flow of food at every stage.

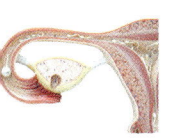

Reproductive System

CELLS

In the human body, the reproductive system causes the birth of a new young one or offspring. It is one of the most important systems in the human body. Different organisms living on this Earth have unique capacities of reproduction.

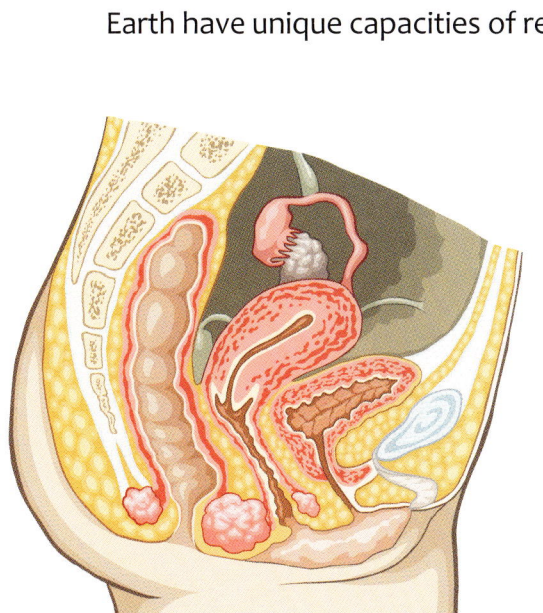

Lateral view of the female reproductive system.

Types of reproduction

Asexual reproduction: Some organisms can give birth to their offspring on their own. Fission, budding, fragmentation and formation of rhizomes, and stolons are the mechanisms of asexual reproduction.

Sexual reproduction: Organisms that have two different sexes can reproduce sexually and give birth to their offspring. As a result of mating, male and female produce their offspring.

Organs involved in reproduction

Male sex organs: The testes, epididymis, seminal vesicles and prostate are male reproductive organs.

Female sex organs: The vagina, uterus, ovaries and fallopian tubes are female reproductive organs.

Functions of the reproductive system

- To produce sperm and ovule
- To transport and sustain these cells
- To nurture immature offspring
- To produce hormones necessary for the production of cells, maintaining pregnancy and delivering the baby

A pregnant woman in her third trimester.

SCIENCE ENCYCLOPEDIA

DNA

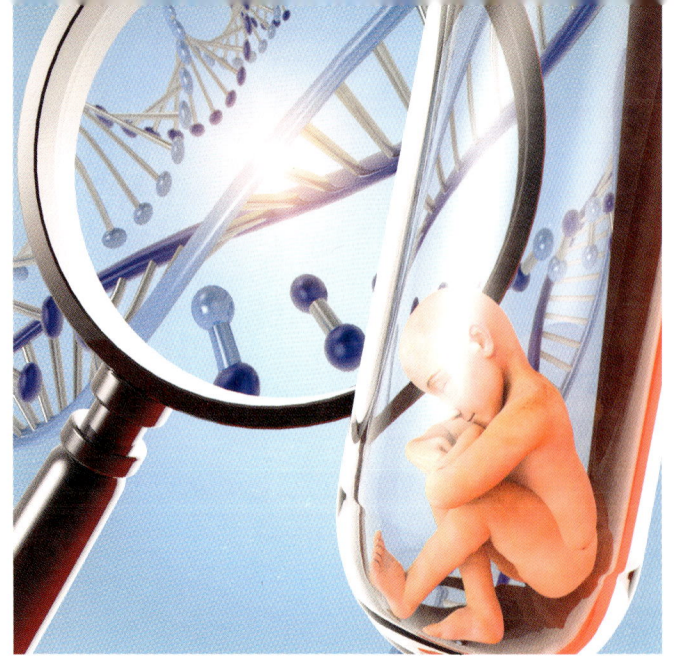

DNA is the abbreviation for deoxyribonucleic acid. It is the hereditary material of all living organisms. You can identify organisms on the basis of their DNA. DNA can be called the biological storage of information. It is a long, linear, double-helical structured polymer found in the nucleus of a cell associated with the transmission of genetic information.

Analysing DNA samples.

Discovery of DNA

The quest for the discovery of DNA began in the early 1950s. English molecular biologists Francis Crick and American molecular biologists James Watson were the two men who got the Nobel Prize in 1953 for the discovery of three-dimensional, double helical structure of DNA. However, the contribution of Swiss biologist Friedrich Miescher, English chemist Rosalind Franklin, American biochemist Linus Pauling and Kiwi molecular biologist Maurice Wilkins should not be forgotten.

DNA location

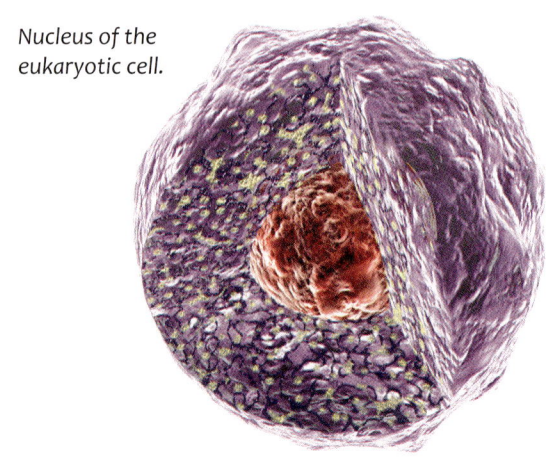

Nucleus of the eukaryotic cell.

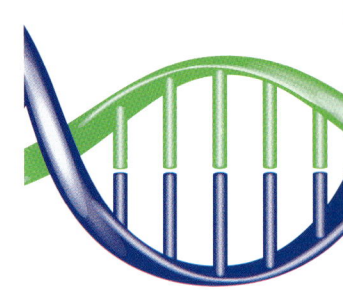

DNA is found in different locations in different types of cells. In eukaryotes, DNA is present inside a cell in the nucleus. As the cell is very small and organisms have many DNA molecules per cell, each DNA molecule must be tightly packaged. This packaged form of DNA is called a chromosome. During DNA replication, it unwinds so that it can be copied. DNA found in the cell's nucleus is known as nuclear DNA. An organism's complete set of nuclear DNA is called its genome. Besides the DNA located in the nucleus, humans and other complex organisms have a small amount of DNA called mitochondria in their cell structure. Mitochondria generates the energy that the cell requires to function properly.

30

CELLS

Classification

Nucleic acid – There are two types of nucleic acids found in living organisms RNA and DNA.

Nucleobase classification – The nucleobases are of two types. The first type is purines, adenine and guanine, and the second type is pyrimidines, cytosine and thymine. The arrangement of the two nucleotides provides the information for building and maintaining an organism's identity. This is called a base pair.

Grooves – The double helix forms spaces or grooves of unequal sizes between the strands, which provides a binding site for the proteins.

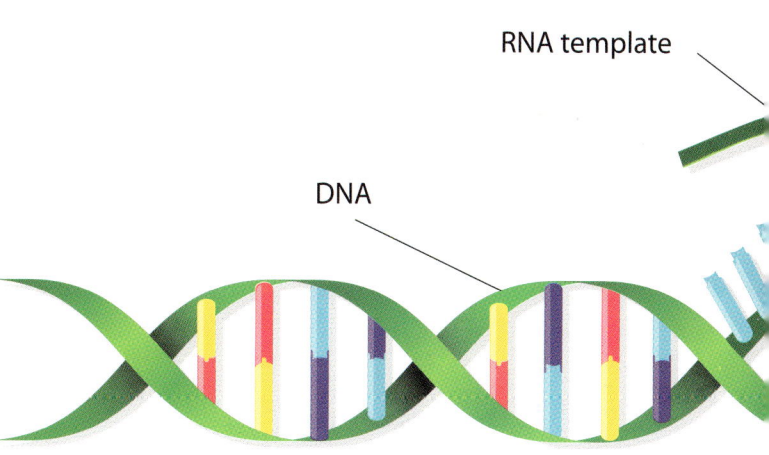

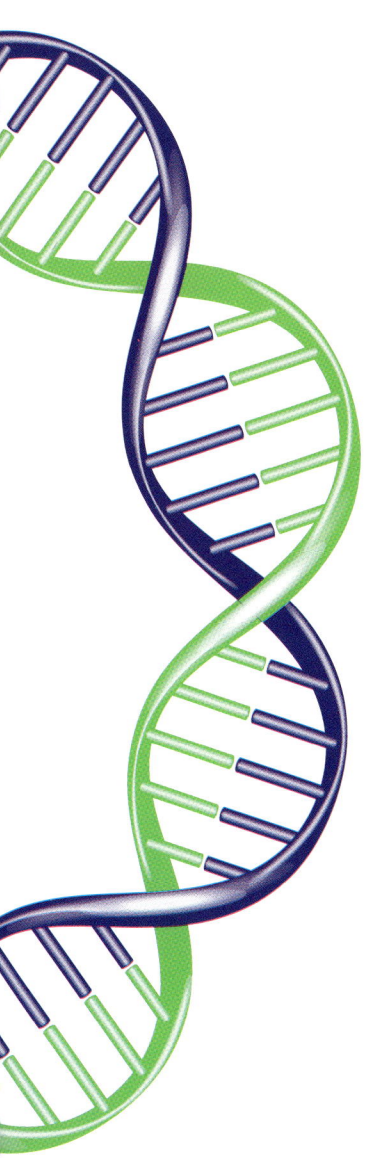

DNA composition

DNA consists of two polynucleotide chains coiled together. Each of the nucleotide is composed of a nitrogen-containing nucleobase with monosaccharide sugar called deoxyribose and a phosphate group. Nucleobases can be adenine (A), guanine (G), cytosine (C) or thymine (T). The structure of DNA is like a ladder with the base pairs as the ladder's rungs and the sugar and phosphate molecules as the vertical sidepieces. An important property of DNA is that it can replicate.

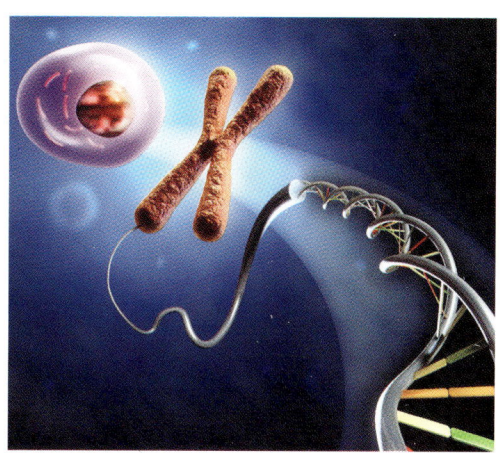
Formation of an animal cell from DNA.

What is the DNA double helix?

The term "double helix" describes the DNA's winding, that is, its two-stranded chemical structure. This shape can be best described as a twisted ladder. The shape gives DNA the power to pass along biological instructions with great precision. From a chemical standpoint, the DNA's double helix's sides of the ladder has strands of alternating sugar and phosphate groups. These strands run in opposite directions. Each "rung" of the ladder is composed of two nitrogen bases paired together by hydrogen bonds. Because of the highly specific nature of this type of chemical pairing, base A always pairs with base T and base C always pairs with base G. DNA's unique structure enables the molecules to copy itself during cell division.

Scientist studying DNA Helix.

SCIENCE ENCYCLOPEDIA

Body Repair

The human body is an intricate structure with different organs working harmoniously together. At any given point, different biological processes occur, like the circulatory, digestive and central nervous systems. If the working of any of these systems gets affected, it affects the whole body. Through their life, a person suffers from at least one infection and that can extend up to dozens.

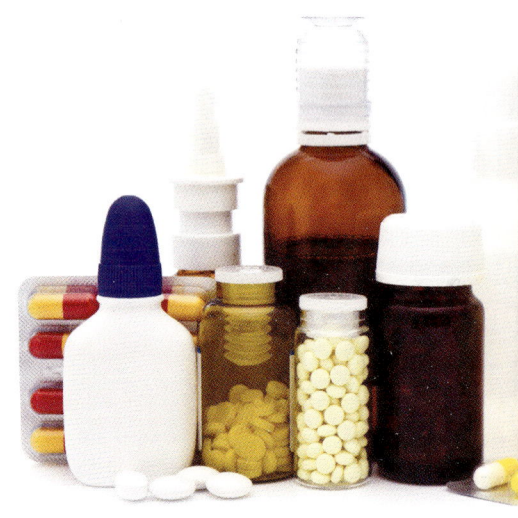

The human body is vulnerable to many diseases.

Different disorders and diseases

Diseases can vary in both severity and diversity, and can affect any part of the body. With the growth in industrialisation and agriculture, the prevailing diseases have multiplied and increased to a great number.

Skin can get infected by bacterial, viral or fungal infections. The nervous system can encounter infections, injury, tumours and degenerative conditions. Structural defects and heart muscle constrictions are cardiovascular diseases. Cancer, tumour, arthritis, anaemia, diabetes and many more diseases have now become very common.

Ancient treatments

In ancient times, limited treatments were available. The doctors had no other choice but to cut limbs off if they got infected. If a person was wounded, the only treatment available was to remove all the tissues and pus from that area, and the process could be quite painful.

Modern treatment

With the advancement of science and medicine, antibiotic, anti-inflammatory, antiviral and anti-fungal medicines were discovered. These are capable of not only treating the diseases but also relieving human beings of pain.

In the modern world, not only can infected body parts like the heart, liver, lung and kidney be replaced, but even the blood of the entire body can be replaced with new, fresh blood. A handicapped person can get an artificial limb attached.

Currently, cosmetic surgery is utilised by many people to alter their physical appearance. Human beings can also undergo sex change with medical surgery.

Naturopathy

Naturopathy is the treatment of a disease by natural means. This field has also made great advancement in recent years. This treatment has the advantage of nil side effects.